The Gift Of Poetry

(Inspirational)

D1365028

Sarah A. Bell

THE
GIFT OF POETRY

(Inspirational)

SARAH A. BELL

ISBN 1-55630-202-9

Published by:
God's Love Overpowers

Table of Contents

Dedication

I dedicate this book to my precious sister in Christ, Louise January, who has stood by me as a priceless friend and faithful friend.

To my three lovely daughters with their nick names Marva Rena (Lost and Found), Gaylynne (Finally Grew Up), Teri Lynne (Baby That Away). My mature twelve year old Granddaughter Tiffani Danielle, who is a blessing to the family, who calls me "Ne-Ma".

This book is also in memory of my precious mother, Annie Laura Hartfield and my Dad, William Hartfield. My mother went home to be with the Lord July 15,1995. A poem "A Mother's Tears" birthed July 10,1995, appears in this book.

Special Acknowledgements

I want to acknowledge my sister Frances Fitzpatrick and my brother, David Hartfield who have witnessed the glory of GOD upon my life and now know; "The three have become one."

To Aunt Lula Sherman, who Mom called and shared in the year 1947, regarding the miracle of the glory cloud that descended out of the heavens that hovered around my head. Last but not least, Aunt Jessie Birch who has been an inspiration to me. Thanks for your prayers and encouragement.

I thank the Lord for Laura Anne Krall (almond tree). It was a divine appointment from the Hand of the Lord Jesus Christ. The Holy Spirit was able to make the connections because Laura Anne and I were sensitive to His leading. From one almond tree (Sarah Ann) to another, the Lord has equipped her and I to help reach the lost souls for HIS glory. I thank the Lord for her being faithful and the sharp business mind which the Lord has blessed her.

Acknowledgements

For the development and production of The Gift Of Poetry— Inspirational on CD, I feel a deep sense of gratitude to:

—my precious sister, Louise January who have never left my side, uplifting me with her prayers and persistence.
— Robert January who I watched grow from a little boy unto a grown man, teaching the Word of God.
—Ryan Rody and family, Ryan heard the voice of the Holy Spirit and came to my first book-signing. Thank the Lord he did, because I thought I had missed it. (ha-ha)
—Brenda Scott, the proprietor of The Product Shop, Livonia, Michigan

The Gift of Poetry

The Gift of Poetry is deep within you, you must go inside yourself
to pull out what He has put in.

The Gift of Poetry is pictorial, you see the mental image vivid, and
you express the gift in script.

The Gift of Poetry actually becomes alive in your spirit and
transcends through your hand—down to your finger tips.

The Gift of Poetry is endless—like Niagara Falls flowing, it
saturates you.

The Gift of Poetry, when it begins to manifest, your day becomes
night, night becomes day.

The Gift of Poetry causes you to step out of your flesh and enter
the state of rapture.

The Gift of Poetry is the creative power which the creator—the
one and only living God has entrust to you.

Where Were You?

Where were you—
> When the earth was formed into motion?

Where were you—
> When the sun was told to rule?

Where were you—
> When the moon was thrown into orbit?

Where were you—
> When the oceans were being filtered?

Where were you—
> When the sea was told to be a tranquil blue?

Where were you—
> When the mountains became fortified?

Where were you—
> When the valleys were laid between the hills?

Where were you—
> When the rocks became a boulder?

Where were you—
>When the canyon depths were measured?
Where were you—
>When the fluffy white clouds begin to form?
Where were you—
>When the rain began to fall?
Where were you—
>When the dew kissed the flowers and said, "I Love You?
Where were you—
>When the grass was sprayed with a flourish of green?
Where were you—
>When the multi-color flowers told the rainbow, "You and I
>have something in common; we have diversity of colors ?"
Where were you—
>When the snow covered the land so white and pure?
Where were you—
>When the stars begin to sing?
Where were you?
>You were in the bosom of the King of Kings and
>Lord of Lords!

He Is Faithful, He That Promised

When tide waters seem to take your breath, and bellows do flow—
    He is faithful, He that promised.
When dark clouds seem to canopy your entire being—
    He is faithful, He that promised.
When fear is so thick and canvases your mind—
    He is faithful, He that promised.
When your spirit becomes hesitant and says, "What's the use"—
    He is faithful, He that promised.
When the silence echoes through your ears and no reply is heard—
    He is faithful, He that promised.
When those that are dear seem distant—
    He is faithful, He that promised.
When you don't know whether to turn to the right or left—
    He is faithful, He that promised.

"I Have Not Forgotten You"

When everything seems dismal and blue,
   "I have not forgotten you ."

When My Spirit seems distant and out of view,
   "I have not forgotten you ."

When you tried the door and it refused to open,
   "I have not forgotten you ."

When the years come and go and you find yourself
still waiting on My promises to manifest,
   "I have not forgotten you."

When you toss and turn during the wee hours of
the morning and others are asleep,
   "I have not forgotten you ."

You must remember the words that I have burned
inside of you.
   "I have not forgotten you."

Only What You Do for Christ Shall Last

Rapidly driving to your job; Rushing through yellow lights and smog.
Only what you do for Christ shall last.
My ebony Hair has turned silver-gray, my-oh-my, another birthday.
Only what you do for Christ shall last.
My children are grown and have children of their own.
Only what you do for Christ shall last.
I look at my watch I have to be at the work-site in fifteen
minutes— my assignment is two weeks behind.
Only what you do for Christ shall last.
I should have taken time to minister to the young lad, but my
manicurist bill was due.
Only what you do for Christ shall last.
I will go shopping today; the mall has a sixteen hour shop-athon.
Only what you do for Christ shall last.
I will witness to my neighbor tomorrow, but tomorrow never come.
Only what you do for Christ shall last.
Twenty years have transpired and I can count on one hand the
people I have inspired.
Only what you do for Christ shall last.

The Birds Orchestrated to Sing About Our Soon Coming King

The Blue birds created in tranquil blue, sing about His peace He
has given you.

The Red Cardinal birds sing about His blood that reached down
and saved you.

The Black birds sing about how He has brought you out of
darkness into His marvelous light.

The Peacocks with their multi-color tail sing of the multi-race that
was birth into existence.

The Yellow birds sing about the Son's (Jesus Christ) luminous
rays that saturate and renew our mind daily.

The Robin Red Breast sings, "Come and lay your head upon my
breast and rest."

The Swan as he graces the water sings, it was grace that led us to
win the race.

The Lovebirds nestled together sing of God's agape love for thee.

The White Dove with its gentle, patient, mild mannerism sings;
how we have been redeemed and our soon coming King!

I Have Put My Seal upon You

I have put My seal upon you; no foe can continue to employ you.

I have put My seal upon you when the stormy weather has caused you to become exposed, discolored, and worn.

I have put My seal upon you when the past tries to allude you.

I have put My seal upon you to recognize and confirm the truth of My promise to you.

How Long?

When the tears run down your face and wet your pillowcase,
  you think—*how long*?

When your mind begin to reflect on the thirty-plus years that have
passed and your prayers and supplication have not been answered,
  you think—*how long*?

When you check the clock on your nightstand and it's three
o'clock in the morn and you wonder what this day will bring,
  the thought emerged—*how long*?

When adverse situations try to suffocate you and steal your peace
and joy,
  you think—*how long*?

When once again your mind races faster, faster and
  you think what is right and what is wrong—*how long*?

You check your clock: it's eleven forty-five p.m.—another day.
  You think to yourself things must change; situations never
  remain the same. The scripture comes to your mind:
  "Beloved, be not ignorant this one thing, that one day is
  with the Lord as a thousand years and a thousand years as
  one day (2 Peter 3:8)." The familiar thought begins to
  surface in your mind—*how long*?

The Door Has Been Open
Can You See—
for I Have Gone Before Thee

The door has been open can you see—
for I gone before thee.
No more doubt and despair. Take the fruit of my
Spirit and plant it for Me, and multicolor souls
will spring up and bloom for eternity.

The door has been open can you see—
for I have gone before thee.
Take the creative gifts, which I have rained upon you:
creative art, poetry, music, and painting and begin to
blend. The blending begins inside of you and there
MY glory awaits to envelop you.

The door has been open can you see—
for I have gone before thee.
Obedience is the key that unlocks reality, and the
precious Holy Spirit will flow full stature within you.

The door has been open can you see—
for I have gone before thee.

Hide Yourself in Me

When strong winds do blow and bellows do flow,
hide yourself in Me.

When your children rebel and are always on the go,
hide yourself in Me.

When your monies are low and counterfeit friends go,
hide yourself in Me.

When your parents precede you in death and your
offspring: family try to steal your rest,
hide yourself in Me.

When your car note is due and your mortgage too,
hide yourself in Me.

While waiting for the phone to ring with positive news
about your life-work to which there is no end,
hide yourself in Me.

Hide yourself in Me; therefore temporal things of the
world cannot overtake thee.

One Priceless Friend

One priceless friend which was given to you from
heaven above; accept your short-comings and coat
them with love;

One priceless friend who sits and listens when the
agony seem endless and over-shadow you;

One priceless friend whose endurance transcend
the scope of time;

One priceless friend who constantly hovers above
your head when everything around you seem to fail;

One priceless friend who knows and sees the
beginning and the end;

One priceless friend who is being formed in the
image of our omnipotent, omnipresent, omniscient
King (Jesus Christ).

The Water-Lilies

The water-lilies arrayed in their splendor and glory don't
worry about today, nor tomorrow.

The water-lilies stay afloat regardless of the torrent
stream and adverse wind.

The water-lilies, so brave and pure, wander down the
stream of life; never wondering what is right or wrong.

The water-lilies with their large, flat, floating leaves know
their needs have been met.

The water-lilies with their showy flowers;
know their destiny.

I have Put My Canopy of Love Around You

I have put my canopy of love around you
that saturates all who come in contact with you.

I have put my canopy of love around you
that transforms minds and transform lives.

I have put my canopy of love around you
so the kingdom of God on earth will continue
to be established through you.

I Have Established Your Settings and Goings

Do not fret when the door is shut—
I have established your setting and going.

When time seems to be motionless,
and you begin to feel monotonous—
I have established your setting and going.

When meeting new friends, and leaving
former relationships behind—
I have established your setting and going.

The Fluffy White Cloud

The fluffy white cloud sitting alone; waiting for
the music composition to start.

The fluffy white cloud said to the moon,
"May I improvise according to the movement
and the vibration of the stars?"

The fluffy white cloud began to sing and all the
hosts of heaven began to join in.

You Made a Vow to Walk with Me

Come rain or shine—you made a vow to walk with Me.
When thunderstorms try to over-take you—you made a vow to
walk with Me.

Keep holding my Son's hand (Jesus Christ) while walking with
Me and that vow you made will lead to life eternity!

"Walking is a form of exercise. "You must continue to
Walk to keep your weight under control," said the Lord.

I See; I See; I See

I see; I see; I see the darts aimed at thee; you must keep your spiritual armor on so they won't penetrate thee.

I see; I see; I see, above all take the shield of faith where you will be able to put out all the fiery darts of the wicked.

I see; I see; I see, remember the battle has been won for you—walk in total obedience unto Me. (Ephesians 6:10-18).

A Mother's Tears

A mother's tears flow at the birth of her child.

A mother's tears flow at the death of her child.

A mother's tears are a cloak of protection
saturating her off-spring from the crown of
their head continuously to the soles of their feet.

A mother's tears reach the highest mountain
and go down into the lowest valley.

A mother's tears tell her off-spring while they're
on the mountain top, "I knew you could do it."

A mother's tears flow down to the lowest valley;
enabling her off-spring to swim out of destruction
to safety.

A mother's tears are like a musical composition,
each note and tear is waiting to hear and feel
the crescendo.

Can't You See and Feel the Hurting People?

Can't you see and feel the hurting people
running to and fro ?

Can't you see and feel the hurting people saying,
"Why was I born?"

Can't you see and feel the hurting people saying,
"A new month with days of rejection, repetition,
remorse."

Can't you see and feel the hurting people saying,
"There is no where to hide."

Can't you see and feel the hurting people saying,
"When will it all end?"

Can't you see and feel the hurting people saying,
"I've lost all hope."

Can't you see and feel the hurting people saying,
"Where can I find truth?"

Truth is found in the *bosom of Christ*
the Sovereign King.

It's a Joy to Give

It's a joy to give, to see the smiling faces and hear the hearty laughter.

It's a joy to give when you know you have eternal dividends.

It's a joy to give, to share your time, to share your creative art, and to share your God-given wisdom and knowledge.

It's a joy to give, to share the Living Word; when you were told, you can't do that and you said, "I can do all things through Christ which Strengthens me." (Phil 4:13)

It's a joy to give, to feed the famished, provide clothing, and provide shelter to the homeless.

It's a joy to give, when you learn to give you are living a fruitful life, and full life.

I See Leaves as Hearts on Trees

When I see leaves on a tree, it reminds me
of how our hearts should be—forever touching,
up-lifting and nourishing one another.

I see leaves as hearts on trees,
I see the love of God looking down
On thee, Whose heart was pierced for you and me.

Said the Sparrow to the Tree

Said the sparrow to the tree, "How tall are thee?"
The tree replied, "Climb upon my branches and see."
The sparrow immediately begin to climb higher,
higher, higher, for nothing could stop his strive.

Said the sparrow to the tree,
"There is no end to your branches
for they extend to infinity."

From Glory to Glory

From glory to glory can you see it's no longer
I, but Christ living in me.

From glory to glory the desires that I had
no longer appease me.

From glory to glory he has put His seal upon me;
no one can pull me out of the palm of His hand.

From glory to glory I was once like the caterpillar,
then transformed to the beautiful butterfly to an
exalted level.

From glory to glory Jesus Christ was sacrificed on
Calvary that set me totally free!

From glory to glory my countenance radiant our soon
coming King!

The Rainbow

When you see the rainbow in the sky it is a covenant of
My love for you.

When you see the rainbow shaped as an arc ,
with it's diverse colors remember,
"I Am the God of many colors
and creeds, and I have met your need."

When You See and Feel the Rain

When you see and feel the rain saturate
you through and through,
*"Remember I am the God who gives in
abundance to you,
and I have rained many blessings
upon you."*

I Have Put My Spirit into Your Spirit

I have put My Holy Spirit into your spirit, therefore we become one.

I have put My Holy Spirit into your spirit and we become joint heirs of our Father's kingdom, which there is no end.

I have put My Holy Spirit into your spirit to give you the desire to obey the living word of God.

I have put My Holy Spirit into your spirit to calm the raging storm.

I have put My Holy Spirit into your spirit to guide you to the open door.

I have put My Holy Spirit into your spirit to lead the captive free.

I have put My Holy Spirit into your spirit that you win souls for Me.

You Are at the Crossroads of Life

You are at the crossroads of life; there are decisions
to be made; will you decide for earthly fame and
fortune or eternal gain?

You are at the crossroads of life, think how your
decision will benefit others, and you have eternal gain.

You are at the crossroads of life, "Me, Myself and I"
are memorized in your mind; then you have earthly gain.

You are at the crossroads of life, there is one decision to be
made, The decision of a life-time; where will you spend
eternity?

The Tide Has Changed

The tide has changed, come swim with me; the rise
and fall of the ocean waves of life were predetermined
for thee.

The tide has changed, divert your hand-stroke,
because your course of life has changed.

The tide has changed, the new course seems strange,
but I have threaded the ocean before you.

Can You Hear the Children Crying?

Can you hear the children crying,
"My birth was predetermined, please let me fulfill my
dream."

Can you hear the children crying,
"My innermost being has been forsaken and my
natural need abated."

Can you here the children crying?
It sounds like echoes in my ears.

Can you hear the children crying?
Their laughter has become small sparks, cascading
down into darkness.

Can you hear the children crying,
"I'm not looking for tomorrow because of the lack of
nurturing and fun activities."

Can you hear the children crying,
"We came into the world but did not know that we
were born to be loved."

Can you hear the children crying,
We were formed in the image of our Heavenly Father
and that image is, "God Is LOVE."

Transformed From a Crushed Dandelion into A Beautiful Red Rose

Trampled by the woes of life degenerated and no where to go—

Repeatedly pulled and thrown aside and told "You are no use for anything"—

Then one day you meet the Son (Jesus Christ) whose rays shined divinely upon thee—

You were transformed and regenerated into a beautiful red rose to radiate for His Glory.

From Discipline to Disciple

From discipline that develops self-control, it's no longer
I that reigns in your mortal body.
You become a disciple; a follower of Jesus Christ.

I Have Lifted
the Financial Burden from You

I have lifted the financial burden from you and cast it
into the sea of forgetfulness; never to remember again.

The Hidden Pine Cone

The hidden pine cone *lying in the midst of fall leaves
and snow; waiting to be picked up and start anew.
Many footsteps have brushed me aside,
not knowing my beauty that lie inside.*

One Lonely Sparrow

One lonely sparrow *sitting alone hunting for food
on a cold winter morn.*

The Spirit of the Lord *spoke to the sparrow and said,
"Go to the top of the tree for I have placed food for
thee; go quickly to receive before adversity
steal from thee."*

The Glory Cloud

*At the age of two my mom placed me in the front yard
and the glory descended; hovering around my head
and taught me what to do.*

The glory cloud *had transfixed my mind, and I stood
motionless in HIS time.*

The Spirit of the Lord spoke through the glory cloud
*and said, "I will never leave nor forsake you and trust
me with your total being."*

The glory cloud *began to show me where I would be in
nineteen-hundred-seventy-two, saved and winning
souls for* His Glory.

The glory cloud *continued to saturate me from the
crown of my head to the soles of my feet.*

When I moved the glory cloud moved. The glory cloud
is God's Glory *manifested in the form of a cloud:*
His presence, His power *and the person* God *the*
heavenly Father.

I Have Enveloped You in My Word

I have enveloped you in My Word—
When you move, I move.
The one thing that moves Me to manifest Myself
in your life is My Word mixed with Faith.

I have enveloped you in My Word—
speak My Word only because My Word is
living inside of you.

I have enveloped you in My Word—
Let My Word walk and talk inside of you.

In Me You Move and Have Your Being

In me you move and have your being—
anything that constitute life.

In me you move and have your being—
*from the smallest ant—to mortal men
and women.*

In me you move and have your being—
remember, I AM the giver of life.

The Constellation of the Stars Sing of My Glory

The constellation of the stars *sing*—
in harmony of my glory!

The constellation of the stars—
are obedient unto my voice; when I call
them by their names.

The constellation of the stars—
can feel the vibration of My awesome glory !

His Eyes of Love

Each person that enters your life; look at them
with, *"His Eyes of Love"*.

Don't focus on their faults but on their goodness.
Christ looked at all with, *"His Eyes of Love"*,

And His eyes were saying, *"God Is Love."*

I Have Brought You Out of Obscurity

I have brought you out of obscurity, *so they will see My Glory resting on thee.*

I have brought you out of obscurity, *so your gifts will saturate souls from sea to sea.*

I have brought you out of obscurity, *so everyone that reads the poems will be delivered and set free.*

I have brought you out of obscurity, *so people will feel, hear, and see the manifestation of the* Holy Spirit *that dwells in thee!*

When You Look in The Mirror, What Do You See?

When you look in the mirror what do you see?
Begin to see the image of Christ Jesus reflecting on thee.

When you look in the mirror what do you see?
"Your short-comings I have coated them with My love,
so they are not looking at thee."

When you look in the mirror what do you see?
"You are not to be sin-conscious for I have delivered thee".

When you look in the mirror what do you see?
"Look for My Son *coming to rapture thee."*

Fast and Consecrate Yourself for Me

Fast and consecrate yourself for Me,
*and watch My wisdom and knowledge
envelop you internally.*

Fast and consecrate yourself for Me,
and you and I will become intimate.

Fast and consecrate yourself for Me,
and people will see My Holy Spirit
resting richly in thee.

Your Latter Testimony Will Surpass the Former

In your distress and dismay—
your latter testimony will surpass the former.

In your disobedience and disorder—
your latter testimony will surpass the former

In your disappointments and discord—
your latter testimony will surpass the former.

In your disbelief and discard—
your latter testimony will surpass the former.

In your faithlessness and faltering—
your latter testimony will surpass the former.

In your failings and fair weather friends—
your latter testimony will surpass the former.

Remember your latter testimony will surpass the former!

The Weeping Willow Tree

The weeping willow tree stands alone;
arrayed in it's splendor and My Glory.

The weeping willow tree also known;
"Weeping may endure for the night,
but joy cometh in the morning"
(Ps 30:5).

(Dedicated to Karen Lynne Dunlap)

Your Thought and My Thoughts Blend Together

Your thoughts and my thoughts blend together,
therefore we will live together for eternity!

Your thoughts and my thoughts blend together,
so you will begin to see super-naturally.

Your thoughts and my thoughts blend together,
so you will know when My Holy Spirit is
speaking unto you.

The Vision Has Been Burned in You

The vision has been burned in you
before you were formed in your mother's womb.
The vision which I have given you will become clear.
The purpose will become known, and it is personal.

The vision has been burned in you.
Use your vision according to MY WORD,
and your life and others will be replenished.

The vision has been burned in you,
and you must remember,
"I placed the vision inside of you—
by Spiritual conception—not natural conception!"

"Before I formed thee in the belly, I knew thee, and
before thou come forth out of the womb, I Sanctified
thee, and I ordained thee a prophet unto the nations."
(Jeremiah 1:5)

In His Silence

In His silence—
  I can hear and feel His Spirit in me.

In His silence—
  I can perceive His instructions for me.

In His silence—
  I can feel His bosom embrace me.

In His silence—
  I can feel His nail-scarred hands directing me.

In His silence—
  I can feel He is touched with my infirmity.

In His silence—
  I know He will never leave or forsake me.

In His silence—
  I have life eternal !

"He was led as a sheep to the slaughter; and like a lamb
dumb before his shearer, so he opened not His mouth"
(Acts 8:32).

Doing God's Will—Will Last

I was chosen to be the senior class president, but,
Doing God's Will—Will last.

I was chosen to be, "The one most likely to succeed," but,
Doing God's Will—Will last.

I was chosen to be the captain of the cheer-leading team, but,
Doing God's Will—Will last.

After doing God's will—you can rest, rest, rest,
for you have passed His test.

(Dedicated to my grand daughter Tiffani D. Mitchell)

Lord Work on Me

Lord work on me,
when surrounded by ignorance to know when to
speak and when to keep my lips sealed.

Lord work on me,
teach me to continue to realize that some of your
children are at various steps of spiritual maturity.

Lord work on me,
to realize in my heart (spirit) that we are being
formed in the image of your Son.

Lord work on me.

I'm Here, But You Can't See Me

I'm here but you can't see Me—
continue to move out and don't doubt in your heart.

I'm here but you can't see Me—
don't be dormant, I move as you move.

I'm here but you can't see Me—
remember all things work together for good for
them who love God, to them who are the called
according to HIS purpose. (Rom 8:28)

I'm here but you can't see me.
...and don't doubt...

There Is No Stopping You

There is no stopping you—
be as the ant working continuously storing
up treasures to minister unto Me (Holy Spirit).

Minister unto Me

Minister unto Me (Christ) first, than unto mankind.

Minister: means to give service, give love and to give total self!

My Soul-mate for Life

My soul-mate for life never has mood-swings or distress.

My soul-mate for life always has positive words
for what I attempt to do.

My soul-mate for life says, "I knew you could do it."

My soul-mate for life gave His life on Calvary
so my soul and spirit could be free!

My soul-mate for life is sweet Jesus Christ
who reigns for eternity!

When You Yield to My Spirit

When you yield to My Spirit—
My wisdom and knowledge are
limitless through you.

When you yield to My Spirit—
My super-natural power shall
flow through you to set the
captive free! Son: (Jesus Christ)

When you yield to My Spirit—
people will see and know it's
My Holy Spirit upon you.

Fly Until You Touch the Son

Fly until you touch the Son and His sun-rays will penetrate you from the crown of your head to the soles of your feet.

Fly until you touch the Son and you will be purged and become anew.

Turn Your Off-spring Loose

Mothers, don't nurse your off-spring from your breast
the rest of their lives—turn them loose and let them fly!

Turn your off-spring to the Son (Jesus Christ)
for they were a loan from heaven above.

Turn your off-spring loose **and** Christ will cradle and
nurture them in His loving arms.

The Poems Have Taken Flight

The poems have taken flight, north, south,
east, west; so the human race can be delivered
from their unfruitful plights and begin to bear
more fruit for His Glory.

I Move as You Move

When you sit and sit with folded hands in your lap
with empty wanderings all nestled in your mind.
I move as you move.

I have already given you the promises based upon
My Word. Get up, get up, get up and begin to act
upon My Word.

I move as you move—and remember faith is the key
that opens reality;

I move as you move!

Annie Laura, My Matriarch Queen

Annie Laura, my matriarch queen was quiet and serene.
Her family always came first regardless how it seemed.

Annie Laura, my matriarch queen made fruitful
decisions for her off-spring while still in the womb.

Annie Laura, my matriarch queen–her daily prayer was,
"Lord keep my off-spring in your bosom, therefore I know
the enemy can't destroy them."

Annie Laura, my matriarch queen lived for her off-spring
as well as died for them.

Annie Laura, my matriarch queen has become a
super-natural holy being.

(Dedicated to my MOM, " Love you, see you soon."
Your daughter,
Sarah Ann)

The Three Have Become One

The three were conceived in the womb of Annie Laura,
my matriarch queen.

A baby girl and a baby boy born in February and a baby
girl in March.
"The three have become one."

When we were small mom kept us together;
two in the stroller and one by her side.
"The three have became one."

A new phase entered our lives, we were grown and
everyone on their own. Different concept of life had
taken root in our lives.
"The three have become one."

The division had set in with the three siblings. Finally
July 15, 1995, my matriarch queen decided to come
to heaven with me so,
"The three have become one."

(Dedicated to Frances and David
the author's sister and brother.)

My Love I Have Given You

My Love I have given you—
don't keep it to yourself;
spread it, so I will become widely known.

My Love I have given you—
saturate your enemies with My love and their
hearts will become new.

My Love I have given you—
has established My fortified protection
around you.

My Love I have given you—
will free the people bound in captivity!

Flirting with the Enemy

Flirting with the enemy
will bring destruction and shame;

Flirting with the enemy
has only earthly gain;

Flirting with the enemy
covers you in utter darkness;

Flirting with the enemy
keeps your heart (spirit) stained;

Flirting with the enemy
will bring a reproach to God's name.

You Have a Decision to Be Made

You have a decision to be made—
where will you spend eternity?

You have a decision to be made—
will you continue to bathe in life's counterfeit jewels?

You have a decision to be made—
will your mind stay in confusion and severe mental or
emotional pain?

You have a decision to be made—
will you accept My Peace and tranquility and live
with Me for eternity?

Yours forever,
Jesus Christ
"I LOVE YOU."

His Eyes

His eyes were watching me as I was being transformed by His Spirit to be used for His Glory.

His eyes were stern and focused on me. I wondered to myself is He going to speak to me. He did not utter one word, but His eyes were watching me. His eyes were stern and unyielding to me.

His eyes pierced my spirit and said, "I will never leave or forsake thee." (Heb 13:5)

The Spirit of the Lord came to me in a dream—it was Jesus Christ. His eyes I will never forget. The year was June 1978 (summer).

Fleeting Moments Are Like Leaves

Fleeting moments are like leaves falling,
falling, falling from the trees. The next day they are
laying on the ground, no longer resembling a leaf,
but just a memory.

Fleeting moments are a short period of time, so
cherish each moment and baste it with God's love.

Silhouette in the Sky

It is amazing to see the panorama of the sky, and the silhouette of the trees extending their branches toward the sky.

They Are Going the Wrong Way

Driving on the expressway watching my speed—many
drivers on my left and right speeding pass me.
"They are going the wrong way"

My heart beating twice as fast (as they were speeding).
I want to cry out, "Can't you see HIM (Jesus Christ)
standing on the expressway of your heart, but
"They are going the wrong way."

With His outstretched arms of love, He cries out,
"They are going the wrong way ."

"Please Give Me the Right-of-Way"

Please give Me the right-of-way to the road in your life.
Follow MY direction and you will have eternal life.
Yield when I say, "Yield," stop when I say "stop,"
make the right turn, and watch the road-blocks,
and watch and pray.

His Search-light Beacons

His search-light focuses high and low
beckoning people to come to the fold.

His search-light moves from His
throne, throughout the universe and
hovers around each one.

His search-light beckons and says,
"My precious lost sheep come home."

Fight the Good Fight of Faith

When everything seems to be dismal and going
contrary to My Word,
Fight the good fight of faith.

When you take three steps toward your goal and
adversity knocks you back six steps,
Fight the good fight of faith.

When you go to the doctor and he tells you,
"Well you are getting older and arthritis has set in."
Tell Arthur, "You must flee because the Son (Jesus
Christ) has set me free."
Fight the good fight of faith (I Timothy 6:12).

The Holy Spirit and the Ocean That Saturated Me

I will never forget when the Holy Spirit came into my room while I was laying down.

I was in a ocean of rapturous delight. The Holy Spirit and I swimming together and the waves as high as the heavens had saturated me.

I actually felt the waves enter into my spirit and soul. The Holy Spirit was directing the waves upon me. The waves were saying, 'I'm here to renew, restore, revive, and replenish thee." Once again the precious Holy Spirit let me know He is my comforter, my teacher, my helper, my friend and He will be with me for eternity. (John 14: 16-18)

One Small Sparrow

One small sparrow perched high alone
early Saturday morn, also know the secret
of meditation and being alone.

One small sparrow flies with the greatest of ease—
knowing the heavenly Father's love and that
He has provided for its need. (Philippians 4:19)

The Love of Our Natural Father— The Love of Our Heavenly Father

From a great distance the natural father
recognized his lost son and was filled with
compassion for him. He ran to his son threw
his arms around him and kissed him.
(Luke 15:20)

How much more our heavenly Father
recognizes you and I when we were dead in
our sin and distant from Him.

The unconditional love of our heavenly
Father draw the unsaved to Him, therefore
we are born again!

Stand

Stand as strong as the trees when adversity comes at thee.

Our big brother and Savior (Jesus Christ) have paved the way for thee; so stand.

Saints That Are Gone Are Waiting for Their Loved Ones

Mothers that have preceded their daughters,
Fathers that have preceded their sons
are rejoicing continuously because they know
their off-spring will soon be ushered into His Glory
for eternity!

My Glory I Have Given Thee

My glory I have given thee to open your mouth boldly and testify of me.

My glory I have given thee to teach My Word with My power and authority.

My glory I have given thee to shine like My Son — Jesus Christ–who dwells in thee.

My glory I have given thee to set the captive free.

My glory I have given thee to radiate My joy supernaturally.

My glory I have given thee to be blessed with spiritual, mental, and physical attributes.

My glory I have given thee to tell others that in Me there is life eternal!

My glory I have given thee to tell the people to accept My Son—He is the door to reality and eternity.

"You Are My Child in Whom I Am Well Pleased"

When doubt and fear try to invade your mind—
"You are My child in whom I am well pleased"

When the enemy seem to have you cornered
on both sides—
"You are My child in whom I am well pleased."

Remember I am with you for I am in your heart—
"You are My child in whom I am well pleased."

The Long Limbs on Trees

The long limbs on trees extended themselves
upward toward Me.

How much more should you extend your life
and give it to Me.

It's Spring

Listen at the small sparrows early in the morning singing, "It's spring, tulips spring forth, grass become green, plant your flowers and vegetable garden for it's spring, spring, spring."

The Soil Has Been Toiled

The soil has been toiled, for you have worked it well,
for I have taught you to work the soil with you hands.

Tell My people to use their hands and lift them up
from their sides, for I have blessed the work of
their hands.

Winning Lost Souls to Christ

Reflect back before you were saved—lost
in a sea of dismay. Waves of spiritual death
overtaking and choking you. You wonder
in your heart, "Why was I born?"

At night you would doze off to sleep and have
the reoccurring dream that you were falling,
falling, falling into a black, bottomless pit and
no one to catch you.

"He that wins souls is wise…" (Proverbs 11: 30).

The Word of God Is Alive

The word of God is alive.
It cuts entering your body into your spirit
and soul, and it cuts as it comes out,
therefore cleansing you. The word of GOD
is like a two-edged Roman sword.
(Hebrews 4:12)

Lord, Where Are You?

Lord where are you—when nothing seem to make sense.

Lord where are you—when doors close in Your face.

Lord where are you—when the sister and brother in Christ are against You.

Lord where are you—when you know the intent of my heart is to win souls for You.

Three Rose Petals

Look at the beautiful bouquet of red roses
sitting on the table. The next day you pass
the table three rose petals are laying all alone.
You think to yourself: the Trinity:
the Father, Son, Holy Spirit.

Open Your Spiritual Eyes

Open your spiritual eyes and you shall see Me daily.

Open your spiritual eyes for I am in the flowers
you plant.

Open your spiritual eyes for I am in the garden you sow.

Open your spiritual eyes for I am in the tree limbs
that sway.

Open your spiritual eyes for I am in the tiny infant that
grows.

Open your spiritual eyes and you shall see Me in the
multi-color butterflies.

Open your spiritual eyes and you shall see Me in the
sparrow that flies.

Open your spiritual eyes and you can see My presence
in everything that grows.

Bathe in My Refreshing

Bathe in My refreshing—for I have seen your toil, sweat, and tears.

Bathe in My refreshing—for I have seen your disappointment over the years.

Bathe in My refreshing—and enjoy your remaining years.

The Quietness of a New Day

Sitting on the front porch in June, I can hear
the diverse birds singing and communing in
their own tune.

Beautiful red birds fly in front of me hunting
for food. The birds are not concerned about the
cars racing down the street for it is six-o'clock,
Sunday morning and people are asleep.

The birds, which God has created, can sense and
feel the quietness of a new day.

The bushy tail squirrels scampering upon poles,
tree-limbs, sidewalks and driveways; for it is
the quietness of a new day.

My God's Breath

You see the results of My God's breath moving the leaves on trees.

You see the results of My God's breath moving upon the green blades of grass that grow.

You see the results of My God's breath moving upon each new born infant who takes it's first breath and cries.

The Living Word

Rebuke me with the living word;

Renew me with the living word;

Revive me with the living word;

Restore me with the living word;

Replenish me with the living word;

Resurrect me with the living word;

and I will lead lost souls to the Lord

for eternity.

A Father's Love

A father's love is felt as he holds the small
image of himself.

A father's love is felt as he holds the small
curled hand of his biological seed—also his
adoptive seed.

A father's love is seen with each toilsome day.

A father's love is seen with his staring
wide-open eyes at me.

A father's love is felt and seen when he
encourages me to take my primary steps.

A father's love is felt when he takes me by
the hand and says, "I knew you could do it."

A father's love is expressed when he says,
"I love you with the love of our heavenly
Father and His love will endure for eternity."

The Two Have Become One

With every Breath, which God breathes through me, His breath is saying, "My love I have bestowed upon thee."

With every Beat of my Heart, my heart-beat is saying, "I will promote the development of our love for Eternity."

With the magnitude of my Eye, I see the creator has formed a sensitive, rapturous help-mate for me.

With my loving Arms, I will cradle you for there is no distance between our love because God ordained it before time.

With my Ears, your soothing voice is like heavenly music saturating my soul, when you are not near me.

With my Hands, they will forever extend toward heaven thanking, and praising God for you.

Our Footsteps were ordered by the Lord and He said, "Whoso finds a wife findeth a good thing, and obtains favor of the Lord." (Proverbs 18:22)

With our Total Being, our spirit, soul, body are saying, "The two have become one." What therefore God hath joined together, let no man put asunder. (Mark 10:9)

> --Dedicated to Married Couples.

"Words to Ponder"

Would you rather be persecuted for My name-sake
(Jesus Christ) or the color of your skin?

Each new day is a gift—
will you open it up with excitement
(to stir to action) or let it lay dormant—
(to put away for future use, temporarily inactive).

> S—sin, selfish
> E—evil
> L—lie, lust
> F—flesh

The word self is also in the word flesh

> F—faithless
> L—liar
> E—evil
> S—sin
> H—hell

So, I say live by the Spirit and you will not gratify the
desires of the sinful nature. For the sinful nature desires
what is contrary to the Spirit and the Spirit what is
contrary to the sinful nature. (Galatians 5: 16-17)

"Words to Ponder"

Our bodies have been super-naturally created,
bone of His bone—flesh of His flesh.

New day, new day, new day, sit and be quiet,
and listen for His sweet, still voice. The Lord will
share His Word with you to calm your soul.

In Him (Jesus Christ) we move and have our being;
likewise we are being formed into His image.

The trees leaves sway to the tune—
Jesus is coming soon.

I have learned to look and listen for humor each day
because the chuckling (laugh softly) helps me make it
through the day.

Fly until you touch the Son (Jesus Christ)
and remember the Son shines for eternity.

"Words to Ponder"

I will not be intimidated by man—for God is by my side.

Grow older gracefully because God has given you His grace.

The word evil is in the word devil. Change the letters around you have the word lied and the word vile.

Be sober be vigilant because your adversary the devil is walking around seeking whom he may devour (I Peter 5:8).

At the present you are limited to mans' natural time. When you enter into My throne—Time will be obliterated.

Thank you for giving me the key to your heart.

Child-like manner and spiritual maturity please the Lord, but make sure they are balanced.

"Words to Ponder"

The Gift of Poetry (Inspirational) has taken
Flight north, south, east, west, for My Glory.

Be as graceful as the swan—for when it swims
I can see elegant motion and beauty.

You study My Word but make sure you hide
yourself in Me (Jesus Christ).

The most important thing in life—winning lost souls
to Christ!

Look at the word—sword; you see the word—Word:
Jesus Christ is the living Word.

Consecrate and deny yourself and watch Me work !

"Words to Ponder"

Time: Gods Precious Gift.
Time: in the word time is also the word me.
(Jesus Christ speaking of Himself).
The time that I have entrusted to you
belongs to me.

Remember: in the word remember is also
the word me. For it is the Holy Spirit speaking
of Himself wanting to commune with thee.

Up, up, up and away, The Rapture is on its way.
(I Thessalonians 4:15-18);
(I Corinthians 15: 51-54)

Look at the Son (Jesus Christ) and you will
never be in darkness.

I have put you in a new Spiritual dimension.

Learn to practice being in the presence of the
Lord and create the atmosphere for
His Glory to enter.

Use your creative mind which I have given thee
and you will glorify Me.

"Words to Ponder"

Use your spiritual eyes (center and core of life)
to see according to My Living Word
spiritually and naturally.

Use your hands, and My anointing will
flow through them.

How can you count your blessings for they are infinite.

Many have gone to be with the Lord, and their
visions and dreams have been decreed.

God has His way (Super—Naturally) to get our attention.

I will have a remnant of people that will praise Me
for we are in the last days, saith God.

"Words to Ponder"

Be a wise steward of the time which the Lord has
entrusted unto you.

Many shall be left behind for they shall not have time
to get ready; they must be ready!

Be still and know that I Am God and watch Me work.

A seed must be buried first–then it will produce; likewise,
we must be hidden in Christ Jesus to reproduce fruit.

I have given you wings like the eagle so fly, fly, fly
until you touch My Son (Jesus Christ).

I have given you My eyes to see, My ears to hear,
My hands to touch, My mind to think, and My feet to walk.

Spend your quiet time with Me (Jesus Christ).

"Words to Ponder"

For I have not forgotten you !

I will use you in spite of yourself
(short-comings, failure). I have seen
your sweat and tears.

Law: Tells you what is wrong.
Grace: In the word Grace is the word.
Race—Christ died for the human Race.

Will you doubt Me again? Said the Lord.

To commune with the Lord will bring forth
profound words—Profound: originating in the
depths of one's being (spirit).

Did not I tell you, "I shall show you My Glory."

"Words to Ponder"

I will continue to commune with the Lord for eternity.

The beginning as we know it is the end to the Lord.

Our works have multiplied and saturated the nation.

In the word dread is the word *dead*. "Who so hearkens to Me (wisdom), shall dwell securely, and in confident trust and shall be quiet without fear or dread or evil" (Prv 1:33).

To ignore God is ignorance.
The word ignore is derived from ignorance.

The presence of God and the power of God are two different manifestations.

"Words to Ponder"

There is no such thing as (time) with God—
God dwells in the eternity.

Time begin with the fall of man.

Stop being anxious for circumstances to
change in your life. Everything is subject to
change.

How can you put a price-tag on your giving,
for it is infinite. How can you count your
blessings? For some are unseen (Angels
keeping you from danger and evil traps).

It's the hidden things in life that you must seek out;
likewise dwell in the secret place of the Most High
under the shadow of His wing.

Stress : You are stretched out of shape—no relief.
Pressed : You are pressed against your circumstance.
Distress : Distress means acute anxiety, trouble.

Prescription for anxiety: Let not your heart be troubled,
neither let it be afraid (John 14:27).

"Words to Ponder"

Jesus said, "Peace I leave with you, My peace I give unto: not as the world giveth, give I unto you.

The Four W's Regarding Money: Be Wise, Don't Waste, Don't Worry, Don't Worship.

A laugh a day and speaking the word of God with authority will keep the devil away!

"Words to Ponder"

BE LIKE THE EAGLE:

E—eager to read Gods Word
A—alert to the Holy Spirit
G—God is your guide
L—live for God
E—eternal life has been given to you

SATAN THE COUNTERFEIT LION:

L - liar
I - in
O - opposition
N - nought: zero of no value
(II Peter 5:8; II Cor. 2:11)

"Words to Ponder"

If you seek Me early in the morning you shall find Me.
(Proverb 8:17)

Habits are detrimental to what the Lord is trying to get
you to do or to get your attention.

Everything you touch turn to gold. Take out the letter
"L" in the word gold you have the word God = The
living Word (John 1:1).

"My words, My words , My words shall continue to flow
from your inter-most-being."

Bathe in the moment; Rest in my bosom (Jesus Christ);
stop looking at the clock; stop counting the days from
the calendar.

Your healing is at the door. I have healed you from
the inside out.

Don't let depression or pressure creep in again.

Don't divert your path or course which I have
ordained for you.

In the word SEE are the two letters: EE. We see with
our two natural eyes, but we must see with our
Spiritual Eyes, and that lasts for Eternity.

"Words to Ponder"

Enjoy the Refreshing which I have given you.
(Psalm 23:3)

(Re-store, Re-fresh, Re-vive, Re-new, Re-plenish.)

The Morning Glorys (Flowers) wake up and
sing the praises of the King (King Jesus).

Satan is whispering in your ear, "Fear." The word
ear is in *fear*. Remember: God has not given us the
spirit of fear; but of power, love, sound mind (healthy
mind) (II Timothy 1: 7).

Don't let the Past allude you (suggest, hint at,
Allusion) you. Past: P: Pressure, A: Adverse,
S : Satan, T: Traps.

Indecisiveness is Lethal to accomplishment. There is
a time limit on how long you can consider which way
you want to go. You can't wait for things to happen
to you. You must make things happen for you.

Life as we know it is a shadow of things to come, so
be still, be still, be still.

"Words to Ponder"

My daughters are choosing Mr. Less, instead of Mr. Best, likewise my sons are choosing Ms. Less, instead of Ms. Best.

The days as we know them are already gone. We are here for just a moment…

The word *ear* is in the word *hear*. Hear what the Holy Spirit is saying to the church (Isaiah 55:3).

Incline your ear; come unto me: Hear and your soul shall live; I will make on everlasting covenant with you…

The Lord always Re-invents Himself. That means we are to Explore new horizons, new surroundings, new God-centered ideas.

Everyone is concerned about losing weight—who is concerned about losing the weight of Sin that has you in bondage (Hebrew 12:1).

"Words to Ponder"

Be a wise Steward of the Time I have
entrusted unto you, said the Lord.

The test of a man's soul is when he is
alone with the Lord and enjoys it.

The year 2004 the Lord spoke this to my heart. "You
are in the last lap of your life as you know it,
surely you can make it now." (Lap: Race-Course
Section of a journey).

You were born for such a time as this.

Definition for Halloween: The devil tricks you, the
devil treats you, then leaves you holding the bag.

There is no such thing as daylight saving time. Man
has always tried to control My time.

I have given you a new lease on life.

I have set a burning fire in you, which cannot
be extinguished.

I have given you your stamina back.

"Words to Ponder"

I have given you three C's: Stay Calm, Cool, Collected in Christ name.

The Tide has changed.

MOM: Spelled Upside down spell
WOW: The acronym for Woman Of War.

Female Preachers
    Deborah: Prophetess, Judge (Judge 4:1-10, 13-24)
    Esther: Crowned queen, she risked death
        Esther 4:15-17)
    Mary Magdalene: (Matthew 28:5-7)
    Mary: The mother of James, Jesus

The word *hid* is in the word *hind*. Stay hidden in Christ Jesus, and He will make your feet like Hinds' Feet (II Samuel 22:34). He make my feet like Hinds' feet and set me upon my high places. I have given you Hinds' feet to jump hurdles over obstacles.

Did not I tell you to stop sacrificing the children? I will always have a Ram in the bush (Genesis 22:13). The Ram: The Lamb illustrates the substitute sacrifice of the Lamb of God = Jesus Christ.

Warn the people, warn the people to get saved. Everything else they are involved with is frivolous; If I'm not the author and Finisher of your Life. Frivolous: silly, flighty, foolish, empty - headed, shallow, not serious.

"Words to Ponder"

CELEBRATION OF RENEWED LIFE

Dedicated to Shirley Murray. She went home to be with the Lord April 24, 2006. The acronym the Lord gave me for the word Celebration:

C—Christ the beginning and ending...(REV. 1:8)

E—Eternal life, Everlasting life (I John 5: 11)

L—Love cover all sins (Proverb 10: 12)

E—Emmanuel: God with us (Matt 1: 23)

B—Behold the Beauty of the Lord (Psalm 27: 4)

R—Righteousness from death (Proverb 10: 2)

A—Angel sent from the Lord (Psalm 91: 11)

T—Trust in the Lord (Proverb 3: 5)

I —Immortal : Be patient... seek immortality
        (Romans 2:7)

O—Overcome by the Blood of Christ (Rev. 3: 5)

N—Name written in Heaven (Rev. 3: 5)

(Sister Shirley's name is written in Heaven. Is Yours?)

"Words to Ponder"

"Daddy knows, Daddy knows, Daddy knows". I was driving, heavy burdened; I begin to cry; then the Lord spoke to my heart and said, "Daddy knows, Daddy knows, Daddy knows."

The Lord let me know He felt what I was feeling, and He is, "My Daddy," and He will never leave nor forsake me.

(That is a "Personal" experience. I will never forget, also that is for every believer, because "Daddy knows, Daddy knows, Daddy knows." (The year was 2003).

Notes of Reflection

Notes of Reflection

Notes of Reflection

Notes of Reflection

Notes of Reflection

About the Author

Sarah A. Bell was born in Omaha, Nebraska. Her mom placed her in the yard one warm day. She was two years of age. Sarah's mom witnessed a small white cloud descend from the sky, and begin to hover around her head. Her mom began to call her, "Sarah Ann, Sarah Ann," but the Glory of God had come down and saturated her. She was listening to the voice of God. Suddenly, she turned toward her mom and said, "Mom, I'm talking to the Lord."

In the Word of God is the confirmation to what was established in Sarah's life. Exodus 34:5—And the Lord descended in the cloud, and stood with him (her) there, and proclaimed the name of the Lord. Isaiah 11:6... And a little child shall lead them.

She began to teach the Word of God at various churches in Detroit. Doors were opened to her to minister at City County Bldg, 36Th District Court, Wayne County Community College, and at the Florent Gillient Hall Domitory at Marysgrove College in Detroit, MI.

Sarah Teaches the Living Word of God at the Northwest Branch YWCA, 25940 Grand River in Redford, MI. 48240 Sunday at 1:00 P.M.

The Gift of Poetry (Inspirational) book was birthed from Sarah's intimate relationship with the Lord, Jesus Christ, and being sensitive to the leading of the Holy Spirit, and her personal experience with life.

Accomplishments

- National Library of Poetry, 1996 (Editor's Choice Award)

- Poetry Reading CATV 15, Southwest Library, 1998

- Poetry Reading, 1440 AM WQBH, 1999

- The Gift of Poetry Inspirational, 1997 (Published by Brentwood Christian Press)

- William Tyndale Bookstore, 1998

- Up Close 1998: African American Booklist (Published by Detroit Public Library), Feb., 1998

- WLQV 1500 AM Radio Broadcast 2003-2006

TO CONTACT AUTHOR, WRITE
SARAH A. BELL
P.O. BOX 380893
Clinton Twp, MI 48038
586-263-5679
Email: Godsloveoverpowers@gmail.com
www.thegiftofpoetryinspirational.com

Printed in the United States
129591LV00003B/1-225/P